THE BIG BOOK OF AUTOCORRECT FAILS

Published in 2014 by SevenOaks

Copyright © 2014 Carlton Books Limited

A CIP catalogue record for this book is available from the British Library.

ISBN 978-1-78177-177-8

Printed in the UK by CPI Group (UK) Ltd, Croydon, CR0 4YY

THE BIG BOOK OF AUTOCORRECT FAILS

TIM DEDOPULOS

SEVENOAKS

Introduction

In these days of superfast digital communication, never has the phrase "shoot the messenger" been more relatable to so many people, all over the world. No sooner had the predictive text feature been added to most smartphones around 2007 than the hilarious global phenomenon of "autocorrect errors" boomed too. In the time it takes to press SEND, the entire world went from being obsessed with sending messages to being obsessed about the alarming errors that can occur *when messaging*. And for good reason too.

Just like to calling your history teacher "mom" every day, sending embarrassing messages has become just another one of life's ritual humiliations. But, unlike calling your history teacher "mom" – which is *your* fault – when it comes to a message sent in error, you should always blame your phone's stupid autocorrect feature.

In fact, by the time you've finished reading this sentence, tens of million messages will have been sent, many of them, no doubt, in error and with some truly outstanding autocorrect results. And that's where we come in.

The mammoth tome you are holding in your hands is the best of those brilliant mess-ups; a truly bonkers collection of some of the world's greatest examples of messaging meltdowns and autocorrect bungles, belly-flops and fails – all caused by momentary lapses in attention, drunkenness and your so-called 'smart' phone!

Read each entry carefully, study them and make sure you don't suffer the same misfortunes other poor souls have. And, for goodness' sake, be especially careful when using the words duck, aunt, election and tentacles.

YOU HAVE BEEN WARNED.

Enjoy!

Did you get anywhere with Kasey?

Eh not really, it was nice tho

She was a little cuddly over the popcorn during the movie

I took her home and killed her in front of her place, that's it

Whoa, dude. Brutal.

Huh? Fml kissed kissed, no killing

Please wait where you are. An officer will be with you shortly.

I loved that pasta sauce you did last night! What's the secret?

Hey, thanks. It's pretty simple. Sautéed onions, bacon, peas and cream mostly, with a little stock.

Finish it up with a whisked egg, garlic, oregano, and plenty of freshly crushed black people.

WHAT?

Oh lord. I could just sink into the floor right now. PEPPER.

That was nasty.

I want to kick your puppy.

kick your puppy.

OMG freak.
Leave me alone.

no no no.

dammit pole no why?

hello?

Hi mate, Can I get a bit of a sub from you for a fortnight? No longer, promise.

What's the problem?

I'm down £250 on this month's Realdoll payment.

Sex dolls? Wait, this month's payment? How much do you owe?

Aaaaaaaaaaaaaaaaaaaaaaaaa

RENTAL

Why is that even in my phone? What the f**k? It's for the rent. My landlord is getting narky.

What about your sex doll?

I DON'T HAVE A SEX DOLL!

So that's why you're buying one!

Hey, you want anything for tonight?

Nah, I'm all set. Just you xx

Cool. I got pregnant.

WTF????

ROFLOL!! Pringles, babe. Don't worry. I got Pringles.

Oh. My. God.

That is too awesome.

Aargh!

Good news!

Oh yeah? What's up?

You were adopted.

What? Is that some kind of sick joke? How would that be GOOD news, Dad? OMG, why are you texting me this? Holy moly, you MONSTER!!!!

Not adopted.

Accepted. To Brown. Sorry sweetie, didn't mean to startle you.

You just ruined my makeup!
God. I'm a total mess now. It's amazing I didn't grow up some serial killer.

There's still time, sweetie.

Can you get the notes for me?

Cmon, it would take forever

Just take photos and send

What you need?

The porn

Nooo! The poems!

LOL

cmon, i'm a geek ok

Did you ever see the original Star Wars movies then?

Yeah of course

O Rly? Fave character then?

I love them all, dark vapor and yoga and luke skyscraper and Hans solo it's great

Go away

Is your neighbor still getting to you?

Yeah, he's such a slob. His lawn is a trainwreck, there's a junker in his drive, and he's still got a huge dead walrus nailed to his door from xmas

EW!

lol wtf? Wreath

You know what would be good right now?

One of the Grove's chicken steaks

Mind-reader. With that creamy mushroom risotto of theirs

And a tall glass of asshole cider

What is wrong with you?

Oh JM&J. I typed apple. I know I typed apple

You can't fool me!

Sax sax wert queer

Mako polish

Kudzu outré plo nnnnn

What?

Kosovo

WTF, are you OK? Are you having a stroke??? Should I call an ambulance?

Oh, shit, sorry, no, I'm fine, left my phone unlocked in my bag

Hey, you want any fruit? I'm heading down to the market Sasquatch.

What the heck does he sell? Fruits of the forest?

Hahahaha invisible tomatoes?

How the hell does my phone turn 'square' into bigfoot?

It's possessed.

How's it coming?

Heading off now should be back in a half hour

Great

I sure'd babble booger summer dose Whee not not lime err through mall attack reaper wattage outer

STOP MUMBLING! Even Siri can't understand you!

Anything exciting going on

Nah, just taking it easy, eating some penis

Aaaaaaaaaaa!!

PEANUTS! O m f g! Peanuts, I swear.

Haha right I know what you're thinking about

Nooooooooooooooooooo!

welp today was a disaster. i got cock everywhere but in the right cracks. im covered in it. the floor is a total mess, its under my fingernails, even in my hair. the things i put up with.

thats caulk, obviously.

mia?

Who's the boss?

What's the new guy like?

Seems ok. Kinda quiet, mostly. He seems to know what he's doing.

That must be a nice change. What does he think of your boobs?

Uh..... I dunno? What kind of question is that?

Oh no! I'm so sorry. I meant boss. BOSS.

Oh thank god.

What time is the table booked for?

7.30. It's under the name "Tobogganing"

What? Why?

Sorry, don't know how to turn off auto correct. TOBERGA. Mitch booked it.

LOL

He's pissed about his mirage

Damn auto erection!

Why me? I meant mortgage. I miss my BLACKCHERRYBYGOLDFRAPP

WHAT?

Duck this

Aargh

Hahahahaha

You listen to Goldfrapp

It was good seeing you.

No problem. Think you're a fun gay.

Hey!

Thank you for a fun day. Damn phone.

Hey, where are you?
Pick up, damn it

Sorry. I can't find my mobile. I'll send you a text when I track it down.

OK

Any sign of it?

Not yet, no.

Fair enough. Let me know

OK, got it now. What's up, dumbass?

He gave us like three hours of homework tonight too, the asshole!

Homunculus

o_O

Ahaha what the hell autocorrect? I typed holy shit. What does that even mean?

Annoying morning. Almost choked to death trying to swallow my goat.

U sick bastard!!

What? No. TOAST. I choked on TOAST.

I know u kill lambs. I KNOW U KILL LAMBS!

Shut up!

It's official, baby.

WOOO! I'm so excited! I love you.

No more having to pee on thugs :)

WHOA things not thugs

Good. Peeing on thugs is dangerous. They don't like it.

I'm thinking about getting Tom a death vibrator mask

Death vibrator

DEARTH VAPOR

ARGH

He might like that

Hey! My phone got stolen, so this is my new number. Update your contact lists pls! Love ya! Jesus

Dammit. It's Jess.

Aw. And I thought I was finally saved.

No salvation for you, Dave.

Hey, you got fucktape?

Of course! I filmed it in my basement dungeon back in the 90s, wearing nothing but a barbed-wire G-string and a nasty smirk.

OMG!!! Really?? Syxjroe

Sure.

Ew, Mom! Duck tape. I need duck tape. I gaye this phone.

That's in with the tools.

You scare me.

How did it go?

She wasn't convinced. She didn't like the drapes.

That's inconvenient. What was wrong with them?

I think it's threshold Gerry thing shellfish like.

Uh...

Looks like I'm going to have to get two windows replaced.

What a Odin in the butt!

Last thing I need now is Odin in my butt.

Hahahaha

I know he's supposed to be a dirty old man or something, but that's ridiculous.

I'm going to swing by Kroger and get hard

LOL

Damn it! Gas

Oooh pump me baby, I love your sexy nozzle

Stop it

Mmm, "filling" station

On my way.

Great. I've got a nice, juicy panties right here with your name on.

Y'know, I changed my mind. I'm gonna just get back out of the car.

Whoa. Patty, dude. Just a beefburger.

Just how drunk are you?

Nowhere near that drunk.

This is going to be great!

You're certainly full of Helen's this morning.

Ew! What are you trying to say, perv?

Hahahahahaha OMG beans.

So, c'mon, whaddya say?

Ah, damn it. All right, I guess I'm in.

You're all fart, you know that? :)

All heart

Jackass. I'll be round tomorrow.

What are you like for tonight?

I'm good. Looks like it should be clear skies, huh?

Yeah good night to watch some metrosexual

Uhh, I don't think so.

My God! How did this thing get that from meteors?

Been drinkin'

Where you at?

down a Riptide on 5th. drunk a few beers, did a few sluts, feelin good

LOL yeah, sure you did playa.

shuts

shores

aw dammit

McDick

I'm going to get something to eat. Bring you back anything?

What you getting?

Still trying to decide. Maybe KFC, but my dick seems pretty tasty.

Mcdick!

UGH!

M C D O N A L D S

Screw this phone.

I'm going to get to practice around 7, grab a wrap afterwards, then go curl up on the couch with Dexter and a big glass of wine.

Lucky you. I'm going to be fondling landlady.

Wow. I don't know what to say.

What? Oh, this horrible brick. Folding laundry.

Sounds much less exciting.

Yeah. Also much less gay. And my landlady is an old, chunky, Polish guy called Vlad.

Hey, can you help me with a tech question?

I can try.

What sort of lead do I have to use to plug my camera into my cooter?

Cover for me for a while, will you? I'm SO tired. I'm gonna go take anal in the store room for fifteen.

Haha! That's one way to wake up?

Huh?

Holy shit!

Pmsl

You're evil.

Are you OK?

I don't know. It was terrible. I feel like I died a bit.

I'm sorry, hun. I'll give you a big cuddle to bang you back from the dead.

Wow, inappropriate much? Bring.

At least you got me to laugh!

What you up to at the weekend?

I'm gunna go see the Lord

That sounds kinda final, man.

Huh? No. The LORD

Dayum. Well, it was good knowing you.

L O R A X. The movie

Death might be better.

Babe, what am I going to do?

What's up?

You know what's up, 'ria. It's Mark. Every time I see him, I can't tell if I'm melting or freezing, and then my heart goes into overdrive, and... He must think I'm so stupid. All I ever do is just stare at him like some guilty kid and make mumbling noises. It's got to stop. You gotta help me be less insane. I got it bad, huh?

Huh. Well, you could just try telling me. I've been in love with you for three years, Annie.

OMGOMGOMGOMGOMG

You wanna get coffee after school tomorrow?

YES! OMG.

We have got to find new jobs

Hell yeah lol. What a week, I'm sooo tired I could just drop dead, but I'm all covered in dick fat, and I stink.

Youre what? Hahahahahaha

I don't know what I hate more, you or this phone lol.

You going to watch the match at Ed's?

Nope. I'm just going to grab a beer, shit in my chair and unwind.

What, you're john's busted again?

Crap.

Think you got enough of that already!

Yeah! I scored a girl after class. First one! I snuck through the defense, got clear, and WHAM! I powered it straight in.

It was awesome.

Uh. Goal. I scored a goal.

We're going to have a talk when you get home, young man.

Running late.

What happened?

I stopped by my folks, and as I was coming up the front yard I got hit by my mom's asshole. It totally soaked me. So I needed to dry up.

WHAT THE HELL, CASEY?

Um. Sprinkler. How did that happen?

We need to rethink things. The plastic just isn't going to work out on this one. I think we've gotta get hold of a shipment of those Chinese electronics. Let Arn work something out with those. If this goes south, we're going to scare off Chicago, and nobody wants that. Not even Tommy. So what do you reckon? Can you still get hold of that little Chinaman?

Who is this?

Uh wrong number.

Mom! Help!!!

What is it? Are you ok?

No! How do I get the cooker to 410? I'm trying to cook someone

You're what?

Oh hahaha I meant something, some meat, not human meat promise!!

I hope not!

Sew what?

Can you do me a favor?

What's in it for me... nah, jking, sure

I got a nasty hole I need you to sex

EEK no no no not sex. Sew. A nasty holy in my jeans

Hahahahahahaha

Bring me your nasty hole and I'll sex it up for you

Hey you, do you want me to grab some extra salad for tonight?

Sounds good. Doug's just going to tear through the sluts again.

The what, now?

Oh my hahaha. The sliders.

Although...

Anyway, I'm just lazing around coming

TMI!!

Noo! Combing!

WTF, phone?

I'm heading in to town. I've got to pick up some of Rod's shits from the cleaner.

HAHAHAHAHAHA

Lol yeah, we get all are best turds laundered regularly.

Well, you could bring one of your pies if you like.

Sure, I can do that. How many are you executing?

Only the ones who don't bring pie, so you're safe.

Oh, this wretched phone.

It's OK, I'm sharpening the guillotine.

Do you need me to come over?

Thanks, honey. It's OK though. I can manage, so long as I take things slowly.

I really admire you. So stroganoff.

Are you calling me sloppy? Creamy? Full of paprika?

LOL yeah, spicy and tasty.

Stop making me laugh! It hurts!

Urg, no, I feel like death

Aww. We'll miss you :(

Don't worry, just have fun, I'm fixing myself a hot lemon tea, and I'll have Chuck Norris soup later, so I'll be fine tomorrow

Kick-ass!!!

Erk! I'm sure that would be totally powerful, but chicken noodle tastes much much better

O! M! G! That lard-ass Ian woman!

Man, she's fat and she's called IAN? I hate her already!

Hahahahahahahaha

Awesome description!

Kardashian

She's Lard-ass Ian now, babes

Yeah, come over if you want, but I warn you I'm just flopping around like a slut

Wow, really???

What?! DAMN YOU PHONE. Even my phone is judging me >:(

PMSL

Slug. I wanted to say slug

Freudian autocorrect!!

So excited! I really need more Crumbled ore in my life

What u tryin to say?

Hahahaha can't breathe

U scarin me

DUMBLEDORE!!!!

Still scared

Are you in tomorrow afternoon?

Busy, sorry.

Oh okay. Everything good?

Yep yep. Just suctioning group of kids foreplay.

That's NOT good.

Oh God. That sounds so bad. For play. Auctioning kids for play.

Auditions, damn it.

He's really creepy.

Yeah I know what you mean

What's worse, he's got a stupid little pedophile.

WHAT?

Huh. Crazy phone. Pony tail.

I wouldn't be surprised, tho.

OMG did you see that ep of game of throbs?

What the heck have you been watching?

Hahahahahahahaha

A song of Ass and foreplay!

Truth

Bad news, your father died.

Shit, really? I cremated the old bastard back in 2005, too. He really managed to make that one last.

Wow. You could just have said "wrong number", jackass.

Yeah, at least I'm not telling someone their Dad died by SENDING THEM A TEXT.

You need anything from the store?

Sure. Can you get me some grapes? Pref green and sexless.

^^^ Hahahahaha

Nooo! Seedless!

How come your cakes are always so good?

Secret ingredient.

C'mon, tell me. What is it? Your secret is safe with me.

Vagina extract. Shh.

Aaaaaaaaaaaaaaaaaaaaaaaa
aaaaaaaaaaaaaaaaaaaaaaaa
aaaaaaaaaaaaaaaa

VANILLA

Oh god. I feel so sick!

Not too bad. We had about four inches of rice and the pond flooded the back yard, but no serious damage.

Whoa

WTH? Rain. No rice fell from the sky.

What about frogs?

Plenty of frogs. None from the sky.

OK, I'm in town. Where are you.

Just sitting on the cock.

Jesus! Eww!.

Dick!!!

AGH ok I get it shut up already!!!

Damn this phone. The dock. The dock. The dock.

Riiiiight. "Dock".

Yay!

At last!

New penis!

Uhhhhh

facepalm P C

Yeah, I didn't get that at all. What?

Sorry. Zhang He, dynasty warriors.

Oh, right.

Yeah. That's the trouble with satisfied fingers.

URGH!

Hahahahahahaha. Was aiming for sausage that time.

I bet you were!

You better do what I say, or else...

Yeah? Or what?

Or I'm going to shoot myself in the head with your beef gun.

O_O

OMGOMGOMG! N E R F. I... Just... no

Speechless.

Moody blues

So I was all yeah, I really don't think so, kthxbai

U ok tho?

Yeah, sure. You?

Ehh. I'm kinda moist

MOODY

Jesus K Rist
this phone

OK gunna go hang myself now

LOL

Doing some last-minute pick-ups. Anything you'd like in your stalking?

Hmm. Let's see. A hot vacuum flask of coffee is always good. Some donuts, maybe. Good binoculars. A list of local ladies who forget to pull the curtains. Oh, yeah, probably some sort of night vision video camera thing too. And one of those big sports holdalls so I can pretend I'm just coming back from the gym if anyone sees me.

Ha! You have all that already!

Starving. Can't wait for this to end.

Yeah. Me too. Horny enough to eat dong.

Horny to eat dong.

DONG!

... Yaaa!

Hungry dig.

Later.

Hey sweetie, I'm afraid I'm going to be a bit late. Sorry!

Yeah, it's over.

OVER.

OH GOD IGNORE THAT TEXT

It's OK. Not over. Definitely not over.

Jesus. You scared me.

Sleep well, my dead.

Yeah, right, that'll give me sweet dreams.

Hahahahaha. Dear. Hope you're not dead.

Not yet. I don't like the look of the doll in the corner though

Blow jogs

We'll get you started with running, four times a week.

Okay...

Don't worry, we'll take it easy. Start off with blowjobs.

Oh lord.

I'm so sorry. Slow jogs. Not that other thing.

My phone is insane.

I was starting to worry, there.

Hey, had to go to the corner mart quickly.

All ok?

Yeah, I'll be naked any moment.

You WHAT?

Oooops. That should have said back any moment.

Clothed, I hope.

I'm going to head down the store right now and pick out the biggest, juiciest-looking tampon I can find. The kids are really excited.

ROFL Ewwww!

Oh God. Yeah, that should be pumpkin. That should definitely be pumpkin.

Much easier to carve.

Uhhuh, and yo got a street name there dog?

T-burn

Cool an what number on T-burn?

What? Shit, my address? What's wrong with you? Who lives on a road call T-burn?

Seem you do!

Do you need a new head for your stiffy?

Uh. That's not a question I ever expected to be asked.

Oh haha swiffer.

All kinds of wrong.

Miss you, babe

Aww. You always know how to make me smoke.

I do? Shee-it.

Smile lol

ROFL right back at ya

Did you hear about that cat cafe?

No?

You can go in there and get a coffee and they have lots of cats in there to keep you company

Too cute!!!! I've got to go. I haven't been able to punch a cat in forever!

>_< WHAT?

OMG! TOUCH. Why would I punch a cat?

Cos you're evil. EEEVIL. But they'd call the cops on you if you tried it.

God damn it. The cock I was drinking just exploded everywhere. I'm covered in sticky crap.

Nooooo God! Coke. Drinking coke.

Noooooooooooooooooo

Come on over. Girls' night. We'll get some Chinese, open a bottle of wine, and watch a good child fuck. It'll be a blast.

Nnng.

Chick flick.

God, I hope the NSA aren't reading this.

You're on the list now...

What's the news?

He's on the couch.

No temperature.
He died. Vomit.

Oh no

My god

TYPO

He didn't vomit.

Oh, hell and high waters. I
was so scared.

Keep a lid on it

I tell you, if that cow gives me any more trouble, I'll totally blow my kid.

LID

LID

Yargh.

Classy.

Ugggggghhhhh cant sleep

U shld do what I do an masturbate

OMG

....

Yeah. Not that. Meditate

OMG

So what happens if we remortgage?

Well, you get some cash or whatever, but you also will have that much more to pay off on the house, and your penis will be bigger.

*payments

Huh

He's so full of it. I can't stand damned Hippocrates.

The ancient Greek doctor? What, you got some problem with medical thinking?

STFU

I'm just saying, the whole "don't harm people" oath thing is pretty cool.

Did you hand in your dissertation today?

Uggggg

That's a no?

Yeah. I can't help it.
I'm a big-time prostitute.

Oh sweetie, I'm so sorry.
had no idea.

WHAT? NO! I'm a
procrastinator, not a ho!

I'm not judging.

Can you believe this shit? Soooooo boring uggggghhhhhhhh

Like this one for history, whale foreskin became a statue

Whaaaaa?

 O_O

This thing is possessed. Why florida became a state.

Whoa.

How did the race go?

Not too bad. I would have done better, but I hurt my foreskin. Too much rubbing.

WTH? I don't even...

Haha oh god. Foot skin. My shoe was rubbing.

Now I have horrible mind pictures.

Ya, I'll be out in half an hour

I gotta go slurp my mom

:aaa:

OMG

SKYPE MY MOM

Jesus I hate this phone

You coming to the movies tomorrow?

Don't think so. Too much $$$. What you seeing?

The Huddle.

WTF is that?

Man. The Hobble.

DAMN IT. The job bit. With dildo.

Yeah, seriously, count me the hell out.

Thought I might break loose a bit at the weekend.

Yeah?

Yeah, going to get my child outta the garage and ride that baby into the sunset.

I think I'm calling the cops.

Holy shit.

Yeah, that really should be 'bike'.

What do you fancy for lunch?

Mmm, pussy with lots of sausage.

I really don't think so.

Damn it sausage pussy.

pussy!

You really need to get laid.

p l z z a

And yes

I'm cooking on Sunday. I'm really looking forward to some juicy dick.

You go, girl!

dies. I'm cooking a duck.

Hahahahaha

I have to get a car, something cheap and reliable.

Try a vibrator.

Yeah? Up yours too!

Sorry Volkswagen. Not sure what happened there.

Oh. Hahaha.

Hey, I'm going to go for a workout in a bitch. Want to join me?

Ugh :(

OMFG NO!!!!! In a BIT

Oh God. I'm laughing so hard I'm crying.

What's wrong with Ellie?

Oh. It's sad. A friend of her dads shit himself at the weekend.

So? Oversensitive much?

Oh god no. He shot himself.

Nightmare.

I'm going to hell for cracking up, aren't I?

But what do I do?

Have faith. Pray hard. Trust in Godzilla.

No. Just God.

Hahahaha. The laugh helped. Thank you.

It's snowing!

Woo! We gotta make a sexman

A what?

sexman haha

Oh no, now I imagined it and it won't go away

S'up, Lily?

Do you want to teach me to drink? Don't tell my Dad tho.

Whoa. Sure thing! How's tomorrow night?

Whoa there, boy. Stupid autocorrect. Drive, not drink.

Damn.

You wish!

How's the day going?

Good. Had a fantastic BJ for lunch.

BLT!!!!!

You are in for it.

I have the receipt!

Wow, your vag is really stuffed full today

bag bag bag bag bag bag

I'M SO SORRY!

Nooooooooooooooooo

:P

Kitty-ca-ca

OMG! Your titties are so adorable.

... Thanks?

They're so bouncy and fluffy and cute!

You're freaking me out, Ains.

OMGOMGOMG! K I T T I E S!!!!!

Oh, thank God!

Did ya see Pacific Rim?

Ofc, I live it.

Yeah, I forgot, you're a big-ass ugly monster trying to stomp Tokyo with your insane head-spikes.

Shut up.

Or what, Kaiju-Boy? You gonna poison me with your hideous breath?

You suck

My room still smells of your colon.

O_O

LOLLOL cologne.

shudder

Hahahahahahaha sorry

Hey, how's things?

Not bad :)

You interested in doing some Wurst with me?

OMG. I typed work.
I know I typed work.

Dying here!

You should take Taylor to see the penis

WHAT

NO! What a totally horrible suggestion. This phone is Satan. Pediatrician. Definitely pediatrician

Your phone is a pervert

What r u up to tonite?

Doing my goat

Da fuq????? That sounds terrible

Oh god. WHY, phone? My hair, sicko

I'm not the one with the goat problem

What about Sunday?

I mean, apart from the red erection of Jesus.

Whoa. Bad images.

* resurrection

Oh wow.

Who knew the Lord got morning wood?

Fancy a dump later?

Huh. Not that it's any of your business, but no, I'm good for the day thanks.

Oh ugh. That should be drink.

Hahahahaha. I thought you were turning German on me.

Sure, sounds good.

I keep orchestra

You do????

Yeah. It's not as hard as you think. You just got to keep them hot and damp.

I have no idea what you're talking about

You mean like in a dungeon?????

What? No! Why would I do that?

Oh hell. Orchids. No musicians chained in the cellar.

I could really go for some nice, hot homosexual cookies right now.

That sounds so bad!!

EEK! Home-made, damn it.

Hahahaha

HELP! There's a huge spider outside my room.

It's waiting there for me.

Please get rid of it.

PLEASE

Mom?

Your Mom is already dead, Amy.

OMG! How did you make those sloppy hoes?

It's easy. You only need a paid-up ho and a bottle of cheap vodka. Shouldn't take more than a couple of hours.

OMG!!!!! Hahahahahahahaha

What helps you get to sleep the best?

I love the sound of genital rain.

Erm WTF!

AAAAAAGGHHHHHHHH

Gentle

Not...

... Watersports. Good.

You like cucumbers, right?

Sure

I've got a bunch I fucked fresh this morning. I'll bring some over.

Oh sweet Jesus. **PICKED**

I'm totally speechless

You all sorted for tomorrow morning?

Of course.

Be ready. Your Dad will ride you.

I don't bloody think so.

Ugh. Annoying day. Got held up in meetings, and now I've got to make an appointment to go see the fucktard.

Uh, you mean your boss?

OMG. No, the doctor. How did that happen? My doctor is a decent guy!

Should I get anything particular in?

Maybe some crankshaft juice, if you don't mind?

That sounds filthy.

OOOOOOO. *cranberry

Much better.

Now my cheeks are on fire.

Sounds like you're poking love to me.

Hey. I'm not poking anyone.

Don't text and fuck, yo.

Gah.

Poking fun.

I don't want to know about the other.

Bad day. My condom engine blew up.

Uh, how does that even work?

It's like a steam engine, but you run it on condoms instead of water.

Just feed 'em in and whoosh, off it goes.

What? Really?

Of course not really, dumb ass. CAR ENGINE!

Totally. Last thing I need now is to get dick.

Hahahahahahaha.

Not sure you're right about that, sweetie.

OMGOMGOMGOMGOMG

*sick

Too late!

Oh yeah, don't forget it's Gilberto's birthday on Friday.

Oh, right, thx. I should get him a little girl, maybe one he can eat.

Um...

gift*

That sounded SO terrible.

You're a bad person, your autocorrect is bad, and you should feel bad.

Fancy some dick tonight?

Wow. And they told me romance was dead.

No no no no. D-u-c-k. Roast duck.

So, no dick then?

DEFINITELY NOT ROAST

Hey ma. You've got a crackpipe, right?

I most certainly do not. What a thing to say.

*crackpot

Well! You started it, young lady. I'm not impressed.

No, no, I'm sorry. I meant *CROCKPOT* instead of crackpipe or crackpot.

Oh. You should be more careful with that phone of yours.

It's so cute! Izzy is in the nativity play, and they've given her a little costume and everything. She's the Christmas fart!

Oh! That should be fart

This wretched phone. f a i r y.

Poor Izzy!! LOL

How did it go?

It was amazing!!!!!
He's so cute <3 <3

So I guess you need to learn Spanners, then!

:-O :-p

Hahahahahahahahaha

That's insane!

LOL yeah, I might try a bit of *Spanish*.

What you wanna do?

Let's go out, grab something. Mark's black.

Not cool, dude. He's greek.

FFS. He's BACK. I know he's Greek.

LOL black mark. Not a good nickname.

Are you on it?

Yeah, I'll send a massage to her.

Do you really think that's necessary?

Uh, maybe not. I might make do with just a message.

No happy endings on the company dime!

I have totally had it with you, you skank. You're going to pay for stabbing me in the back like that. I promise. You're going to damn well regret it.

What? Who is this?

Who the hell do you think it is? How many boyfriends have you stolen this week, slut?

None. I think my wife might disapprove.

Oh CRAP. I'm so sorry, Mr. Hooks. I'm going to burn this phone right now.

Who is this?

Hello?

I thought I might go hit up some nature at Tampon Bay

Ewwwwwwww

Just gross

LOL LOL LOL OMG Tarpon!!

My lord.

You'll never guess what Damo just shit in the garage. A freaking BADGER.

WTF? I mean really, WTF.

I know, right? It was trying to attack him and everything.

Christ, I'd attack Damo if he shit me up, too.

O:

God damn

HAHAHAHAHAHAHA

You know, I'd love to blow into your rear hole. Gently of course.

EWW sicko

ARGH No nonononono EAR

So sorry. Horrible typo.

Hello?

You're into the whole clitoris thing, right?

WTH???????

OMG! Sooooooooooorry! Cultural, sweetie. Just cultural.

Wow, your phone

You down Dennys?

Soon

Trying to find a pair of clean cocks

Whoa sorry I asked

I can't breathe

Must be those cocks!!!

socks socks socks

You got a red #2 penis
I can borrow?

Uhhhhh

Pencil

Don't need to borrow
a penis

I don't have a red one
anyway.

But yeah, you can
borrow the pencil.

How are you holding up, lovie?

Urgh. Been better. Still getting dick every morning.

Wow. Lucky Brady!

I can't stop laughing!!!!

I don't think a vomiting wife is much of a turn-on!

Be polite! And don't forget to fuck in that tiny bathroom of theirs!

What a reminder!!

I'm showing that to Tina. Parental orders!

Don't you dare. You know I meant duck.

Later!

I am so stressed out right now I could burst.

I hear you, honey.

I'm almost ready to start screaming.

I should go blow off some steam, maybe go do yoda.

Hahaha is that like the Darth Invader?

You're a terrible person, Ari!!

Yeah, yeah. Enjoy your yoga.

Goodnight love.

Night. Wish I was there to run my tigers through your hair.

Mmm. Hair tigers.

Hunting the wild jungles of my head.

Feeding on the brain-monkeys.

Loon!! (*fingers)

I guessed! Night x

John wants me to see him on Friday

You c**t!

CAN'T! OMFG sorry sorry

We've got to help your mom on Friday

Hahahahahaha

Your phone is so rude!

I'm afraid Uncle David died last night, sweetie. LOL Mom.

What the hell, Mom? How is that LOL?

It means 'lots of love', doesn't it?

Whoa. No. It's Laughing Out Loud. It means you think something's really hilarious.

Oh heck. I've got some embarrassing calls to make.

Hey, don't worry. It was great. My dad really lubed you.

No he didn't!

OMG hahahahahaha

Liked! Goddamned autocorrect!!

Hahaha

Hey hun. Could you grab Tom a-hole while you're out?

Whut??

Tomatoes

I don't even...

Hahahahaha

I'm heading out for a wad

The hell does that mean? Sounds disgusting. Or sick.

LOL. Walk.

Still sounds disgusting!

It's annoying

I'm going to feather out what's grognard

Eh?

Wowsers. Find out what's going on.

Good advice. Beats the hell out of me.

Do you remember that set of tiny screwdrivers?

Uh-huh

Know where it is?

Up in the anus

That's repulsive.

* attic

Hey, don't worry. It'll be ok.
I'd buy you a casket
to live in if I could.

Hm, thanks. Very tempting. I'm
hoping not to actually be DEAD
though!

Oh God! That should
have said castle!

LOL. That's a relief

Miss you xxx

Miss you too. I'm cuddled up with one of your shits so I can smell you.

Gods alive, there's an image.

Noooooooooooo!!!

I really hope you meant shirt :)

I did! I totally did!

ROFL

How's the weekend going?

It's nice actually. I'm sitting here with my Mom and we're tossing back non-alcoholic cocks like there's no tomorrow.

Wow. There might not be, by the sounds of it.

Oh God hahahahahahaha

Cocktails

I wonder...

I think I might have to go for some penis butt + jelly right about now

EWWWW Overshare!!!!

YIKES!

Totally peanut butter + jelly. The other is a total nonononono

Uhhhhh Thank you God.

How was school?

I came sexing in games.

OMG SECOND!
SECOND!

I CAME SECOND IN
GAMES!

Mom?

Ohgod

So what did you think of the new guy?

He makes a great fuck-ball.

You WHAT, mate?

Oh damn. Full-back. How the hell did that happen?

Phone knows what a sick bastard you are, I reckon.

Ah, piss off.

I've gotta get hold of a bigger pussy.

This one is nice and all, I like it, but there's just not enough room for everything I need to carry with me. My hairbrush almost fell out this afternoon.

Uh. I'm thinking you meant purse.

dies.

You should have been there today. The most amazing circumcision.

No thank you.

What? I haven't even told you yet.

Yeah, just no.

I'm not into watching dick surgery.

Oh EWWWW. You!

Coincidence, crazy person.

I know it's a lot to ask, but I'm going to need some help with loving. Could you lend me a hand?

Uh, I'm really not sure I'm the right one for the job.

Awkward.

NONONONONO

MOVING

I am so sorry

Laughing so much it hurts.

I should be out real soon now. Homo from hot lips at last!

Christ on a cracker. HOME FROM HOSPITAL.

Sounds like you're out all ready, 'hot lips.'

Ha ha very ha

So, the bottom line is that they'll be keeping me out for ten days.

We'll fuck.

You wish, wild girl!

* Well, fuck.

HAHAHAHAHAHA
HAHAHAHAHAHA

Hi there, Dave. Do you still have your penis? Mark

Hi there, Mark. That's a question and a half. Why do you want to know?

Well, if it's available, then I'm interested.

Huh. My wife might not be too happy. But do you perhaps mean the Prius?

Yes.

Sorry.

That was a nightmare. I went and shat downstairs, under the kitchen table.

I don't think you'll be able to blame the cat for that one.

What? Aaaaaaaaaaaaaaaa aaaaaaaaaaaaaaaaaaaaa aaaaaaa

S A T

You're filthy.

No, c'mon!

Mom is really fucking annoying.

*MUD

I'm so sorry, Mom. It was a typo, I promise. Stupid autocorrect.

I'm sorry I'm sorry I'm sorry!!!

Mom?

Child is really freaking annoying.

Just drop by the main reception. They have a really obvious slut there that you can stick things in.

Wow. That is a truly hideous autocorrect.

Hahahaha!!

There's a slot. The receptionist is not a slut, obvious or otherwise.

We were in Brighton at the weekend.

Good times?

Yeah, it was a laugh. I got a big chunk of cock, of course.

blink. Very good times, by the sounds of it.

Oh God. A chunk of rock.

You could fry an egg on my cheeks right now.

PMSL

House for rent

Yeah man, he's got a really amazing hooker

Stunning

Umm, good for him I guess? Sounds expensive.

Yeah, half a mil no problem

WHOA. She on like a five year contract or something?!?!

HAHAHAHAHAHA

HAHAHAHAHAHAHA
HAHAHAHAHAHAHA

*house!

I'll be getting into town around 7.45p. If the bus is going to be late, I'll drop you a text.

Kk. I'll make sure there's a taco waiting for you.

Gee, thanks.

LOL! Don't worry, I'll include a newspaper you can use as a blanket.

You're all heart.

You want a big piece of card and a marker pen? Or just the *TAXI?

It should all be fine.

Lets hop

Let's not!

*hop

*HOP

You're just standing there bouncing now, aren't you.

Whoa! Sorry I asked!

Your mother was great today, of course

Of course :)

She turned a lot of heads too, in hers nazi outfit

Her snazzy outfit

Heil Momler!!

Hey, guess what? I got asparagus tits!

tits

Uhhh tits

Sounds nasty. Call the doctor.

No not tits, tits

I think you got asparagus brain as well.

ducking phone

I have to present a class paper.

Yeah?

It's on dirty girls, and what a problem they are.

Wow. Are they trying to tell you something?

Ouch, you bee-atch!!

DIRTY FUELS

Hahahaha

You tried Howie's nuts? Amazing.

No sir I have not. I'll make the effort. I'm quite the penis connoisseur.

AHAHAHAHA!!!

Oh my. I swear this phone is trying to destroy my tarnished reputation. PEANUT, my friend. I'm a peanut connoisseur.

Uh-huh...

No parabola

Sparkle

Da hell? How day Hakeem?

*R*O*F*L*

Duck yard point

Omma just call

You ever try cameltoe tea? So relaxing.

What the hel is wrong with you?

Crap on a stick. * chamomile. Little flowers.

Nasty.

Big dong

What about the group?

Can we meet at yours?

Well, yeah... the only problem is my dong. He's really big, and he gets mean sometimes. Y'know, with strangers.

>.<

WHAA! My dog, dude. My dog.

How bout you?

Yeah, not much. Just washing the dick.

Ah crap.

Dishes.

Yeah, TMI! LOL

Not good. My cock got jammed in the muck, and I couldn't get it out.

??????????????

The hell???

Hajj!

CAR stuck in MUSCLE

Nude

NOOOOOOOOOOOOO duck it

M U D

Not happy?

Y? U ok?

I broke my vag. I was trying to get my water bottle in, and it tore.

OMGOMGOMGOMGOMG AAAAAAAAAAAAAAAA

Sweet Jesus, no. That's hideous. My bag, Ash. My bag.

Holy shit. HAHAHAHAHAHAHAHA.

Gonna kill this damn phone.

Cheesy crust

I've got the Orphan Black DVD set. Wanna come over and get penis?

*Penis

LOL! I mean penis

Yeah, I can tell :(

PIZZA

Insane :(((

Stupid phone,
y u so horny

I'm fat man

HAHAHAHAHAHA

No! This ducking thing. I bet the real Bruce Wayne doesn't have to put up with this shit.

There is no real Bruce Wayne, dumb-ass.

I fucked some lovely zucchini at the market.

I doubt it...

Why? I totally did. Real cheap.

Not surprised, after you fucked them.

Oh this fucking badger-molesting brick of dried fly-turds.

Hey, don't blame the phone. It has a foul owner.

Damn it. Where did you hide the vibe? I'm dripping, and you're not home for hours!!

EWWWWWWWWW
WWWWW MOM!!!!!!!

...

Hell.

SCARRED. FOR. LIFE.

You wouldn't harken to have a 13x9" baking pan with high sides that I could borrow, would you?

Yea, verily do I say that such wondrous treasure is indeed within mine compass, so be ye not wroth, but hasten thy homely posterior to mine humble abode wherein the prize does rest, that thou mayst claim in for thine own purposes, for a time.

Hey! Watch whose butt you're calling homely!

And thanks :D

Front door's locked.

> Go in the sith door. That's open.

Go in the sith door. That's open.

> Dude, I can't do that.

Why not?

> Still Light-Side.

> OMG Hahahahahahahaha

You out tonight?

Yeeeeeeeeeeaaaaaaaaaaaaaaaahhhh oppa gangbang style!

!

hangs head in shame

GANGNAM, obviously.

Mmm, gangbang style. False nails and some nipple-rouge?

Don't forget the tattoos

195

Hey.

Doodie.

*doodie

OFF

DOODIE

Stop calling me that!

I give up

Bro.

I'd kill for some pulled pussy

What the hell?

What does that even mean?

Oh Christ

Pork. Pulled pork

You scare me

Ah, you're going to make me cry.

I wish... If things were different, I'd be with you in a heartbeat. But you're just so fat

FAR!!!!!!!!!!!!!!

God damned freaking phone. You're utterly gorgeous in every way. Definitely not fat. Not that I'd care if you were.

Keep digging...

LOL

Thanks for a fun afternoon, Matt. We all had a great time. Kira and the kids were really impressed with your magic dick too - you'll have to show us more next time!

Hm. That really didn't sound good, did it?

I meant magic trick, for the record.

I don't know whether to laugh or shriek!

How you fixed for tomorrow?

Could do two hoes for $40, say 2-4pm.

Whoa. That's some seriously cheap ladies.

hours

Uh oh. So what did you do?

I broke the remote

That's not so bad, surely

You really mean that?

I'm certain you'll be forbidden

Damn it, you're supposed to be helping.

OMG sorry, tupo. Forgiven.

Even your phone thinks I'm screwed :((

When do you get off work?
My c**ts starving

AAAAAAAAAAAAAAAAAAAAAAA
AAAAAAAAAAAAAAAAA!!!

Aaaa indeed!!!
T damn M I!

I'M KINDA STARVING

OMGOMGOMGOMGOMG

Worst. Correct. Ever.

Hahahahahahahahaha.
Freudian typo!!

Ugh I hate dealing with those car mechanics.

I swear I tried to explain but the guy in there just looked at me like unwashed nuts.

Damn it Siri.

Like I was nuts.

OMG! Noooooo! Ground black pepper. That was horrible.

LOL!

Will you be my Wolverine?

The snarly, stinky rage-beast animal, or the emotionally-crippled superhero? 'Cos I'm not loving either of my options, I have to tell you.

Aaahahahahahahahahaha

*Valentine!!!!!!!!!!

I dunno, after that Wolverine slur...

:)

I'm going to be doing a pan of lasagna. Maybe you could bring some Taliban bread?

I'm not sure. Afghanistan is a long way out of my way, y'know? Plus I'm not sure that you really want a loaf that's sworn to kill us infidels. Could be risky.

* Italian

Much safer, yeah. Good idea.

Al said you might know where to source some stage rigging.

Hm. I can't think of anything available before next week. Sorry, dude. I'm not sure what to suggest, other than to wish you luck with your c**t.

Whoa. *HUNT.

Seriously sorry, man.

Yeah, OK. Thx

Now I really want a rubber fuck

OOO

FML

*duck

R O F L ! Have you tried the Castro?

Yeah yeah, ha ha.

Not much. Chilling. You?

Getting ready for my grandma's sex teeth.

OMG

Sixtieth. She's 60.

Oh god the images go in but they don't come out

You telling me?
AAAAAAA

I'm seeing it at 3.

Don't forget to check it has arctic condom

Yeah, I'm hoping not seem like a crazy cat lady.

Hahahahahahaha

This phone is insane

Airconditioning

Dude, I found this smokingly awesome vid today.

It had this really gorgeous chicken handcuffed to the bedposts.

Wow.

YOU SICKO!

I don't even...

Oh nononononono.
*CHICK.

Ha, yeah, right. YOU ARE CHICKENBOY

Hell, no. Don't do that

CHICKENBOY FOR LIFE!!

We should go grab a bear some time.

That's one of the most frightening suggestions I've ever heard. RRRRRRRRRRRRRRRR... MUNCHMUNCH... Aiiiiiiii!!!

How about a beer instead?

Where's your sense of adventure?

The bear ate it.

I should be back in a couple hours. Sorry. Just help yourswelf then poo the rest in the oven.

...

OMG! Uh, yeah, pop the rest in the oven. Hahahahaha.

So no crapping in the kitchen appliances?

Yeah, that's nasty.

Yeah, I tried that once and my piece of ballsack just kinda disintegrated into shreds.

OUCH

Damn!

Ballsack

Enough, dude.

B A L S A

OK, I just puked up outside your place.

WTF? Why are you such a jerk??

*pulled up

Relax, no vomit

Oh. Um, sorry.

:P

I'm going to go do some shoplifting. Anything you want?

Wow. How about some expensive jewelry?

Oh dear. That should say shopping. I'm going to pay. Well, your father is going to pay, anyway.

Doesn't he always? :)

You should have seen Jessica's rectal performance. Beautiful.

Talk about multi-talented.

Oh God hahahahaha *recital

Maybe for the best. She seems a bit shy for anal porn.

XDD

Ugh. I feel like a used towel. How are you doing?

Nasty. I woke up with a massive hedgehog and it just won't go away. It's crushing me.

Wow, that really is massive. U better call pest control

Ugh, you think they can help?

It's your only hope!

I can smell you from here, you skank!

Uh...

Ohcrap. NONONO! NOT YOU!!! I'm really sorry, Hazz. I meant to text that to my friend Hailey

LOL. No worries.

FML, Hail. I just texted a hideous insult to Harry instead of you. He's got to think I'm a real bitch or a space or both. I've really screwed it up :((I'm never going to get him to date me now :'(((

Wrong number again, Sherry. It's still me. So, uh, how about a date then? :)

The salmon was great, and it came with these amazing butthurt potatoes.

...

BWAHAHAHAHAHAHAHAHAHA

"Oh man, I can't believe you peeled me and dipped me in hot water. You're SUCH a traitor."

LOL

Still laughing. *buttered

You seen jack the giant slasher?

Like some big ripper?

What?

What do you mean what?

What???

You're very strange.

All right. I'll let it slip this time

If you even breed funny, you're in trouble

NO

*breathe

If you breed in ANY way, you're in worse than just trouble

... can I laugh?

No.

Ugh.

This car is driving me crazy. I gotta go get my tits balanced.

!!!!!!!

FFS! My tires.

Hahahahaha

Hey dude, we're going blowing. You wanna come with?

Uhhhhhh not so much, no

Holy crap

Yeah definitely not that. Bowling

That's definitely a much better offer

Are you coping with the math?

It's really hard, like the man sausage

O.M.G!!! *said

Hahahaha I know where your mind is!

You anywhere near town?

Ofc. What d'ya after?

:) I need some bits of dowel, and some 5" Nazis

Tall order, sweetie. Or, rather, really really short order

Hahahaha Just go down that shitty biker bar with a shrink ray!!

Or nails will do.

I like Valentines day. It's nice to stop and anal receive your love one

!

Omgomgomgomgomg

*APPRECIATE

My phone is sick

Hahahahahaha

AAARRGGGHHH

What's up?

My house is totally infested with anus. I've got to find the mound and burn it out or something.

Aiyiyi!! I have no idea what you're talking about, but it sounds HIDEOUS

Oh my God! ANTS!!!

Hahahahaha. Thank God.

Oh man, I had to told her rate some Sirius ash holes at work today. Really mad Denning.

There's nothing I can say to that.

Flapping horse ship.

I hate you phone.

LOL LOL LOL!

Hey, we got any crack in the fridge?

*crack

The hell? I'm damned sure I typed crack

Look, I don't want crack. Crack is bad. I'm trying to ask about poultry.

You know, the stuff KFC sells. Crack.

FML. That damn brother of mine has been at this phone again.

C H I C K E N.

Ha! Damn you, Brent!!!

I'm sorry, Todd can't reply to you right now, as he's dying of laughter.

Had the most insane customer ever today.

I mean, he had a nose and hair, but apart from that he was totally cold emote.

Vole demoted

Whoa!

Hahahaha. Voldemort. There, got it.

Terrifying appropriate! Well, not the vole thing.

Hey, you'll love this one. What color do kittens love the best?

Don't know

Pure rolls!

Damn. Pietro!

Puerto

P-U-R-R-R-P-L-E

Hahahahahahahaha. But not for the joke!!!

I miss you too, but at least I've got your black shit to cuddle. The smell reminds me of you.

O.O

NOOOOOOOOOOOOOOO

Ohmigod. I'm so sorry. SHIRT. Your black shirt.

collapses in relief

Whooo baby, you give love a baboon.

Damn you, Leland.

What? Why? I'm only trying to say you're cute.

What, so you like purple-assed monkeys, you freak??

Holy shit. YOU GIVE LOVE A BAD NAME

So do you!!

Will you be long?

Just a half-hour or so

Ok. I farted dinner

Yeesh. You saying I should pick something up?

OMG! Hahahahahah no no. *started

Ugh. Now I want to punch someone. You gotta remind me to never read the damn condiments.

That must be some seriously annoying ketchup

...

*comments

LOLOLOLOLOL

DAMN YOU, SAUCE!!

Mmm. Beef vaginas

@_@ Aaaaaaaaaa aaaaaaaaaaaaaaaa

Omgomgomgomgomg hideous

*Fajitas!!! Satans own auto cucumber

FFS

Aaaaaaaaaaaaaaaaaaaaaaaaa

So. Wolverine or Batman.

Well duhhhhh. Bar man

Hahahahahaha Yeah, you mean they're going to just go get trashed together afterwards. It would be a serious tab

Holy autocorrects, Bar man!

Quick, Robin! To the mobile bar! Make mine a double!!

Gay milk
Hey Ed, could you grab me some milk?
Sure thing. What type?
4% homosexual
Homosexual
Uhhh... Slightly gay milk??
Damn it. Homogenized

How about if we meet up an hour before?

Sure. It would be nice to catch up a bit. We can have a decent shart

Christ, I hope not!

Hahahaha *chat. I don't know about the other.

Do not look it up. You don't need that in your head!

Gotta pump my tired

Tired

Ahhh! Stupid euro cockrocket

Wow

I give up

I gotta barfed up this phony.

The hall? Change!

*charge

Hahahahahahahahaha

I fink ink hate this piece of schist

You should really turn that autocorrect back off

Yaffle

Could you out some beefsteaks for tonight?

I don't know, sounds a bit cruel. I mean, are they ready for it? Maybe they're scared of how their parents are going to react.

You lost me.

It could be they're in the closet for a reason. You ever think about that, huh? I THINK NOT!!!

Or I could just cut your steaks instead.

Ohhhhh Hahahahaha

Kid-iots

Hi love. Been to collect the idiots yet?

Sorry, pa. I think you meant to send that to Mom.

Oh yeah, thanks.

HEY! Are you calling us idiots?!

You have to ask? Like I said...

I'm gonna bake a lie for Kim's birthday

lie

My phone is possessed. * LIE

*CAKE

ROFLLLLLLLLLLLLLLLLL

I swear I was typing lie!

ca ke

Your phone knows the truth!!!

I had some awesome MONSTERRR claws in garlic butter last night

-_- What the hell was that?

*lobster

Mmm. Monster claws

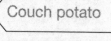
Been a hard day. Just gunna lie on the cock and vag out

Oh FML. Nonononono. Et tu, phone? *couch **veg

pmsl

Hate you phone.
Hate hate hate hate hate

Phone hates you too, Edie

Miss you

Miss you too

All I seem to be able to do is shit and think of you

Uh... Thanks?

OMG!!!!!!!!!!! *sit!!!!!!!!!!!!!

Hahahahaha

Yeah, she's allergic to wasps

She's OK though, don't worry

Just gave her a shot from the epic penisr

WHOA. Overshare! Also, how is that supposed to help?

:facepalm:

Epi pen

Oh man, I love it. I got some free time, there I am, rimming me some guys

Aaa!! NONONONONONO *skys *skys *skys

You. Sick. Pig.

Noooooooooooooooo ooooooooooooooooo

Feel dreadful.

You ok?

Not right now. Mu whole head is stuffed with rum.

?? Alky!

Oh go away. Don't mock the affliction. Flem.

Hey, you feel like coming with for a warty donger tonight?

Um, not really.

Hahahahaha how the hell? Early dinner!!

You scare me!!

Hell, I scare ME.

Good news. The power is back up and ruining.

That's what power does!!

Urrrrrr. Wookie up early. I'm really tired.

> It's more like Mmuuuuuuuuuuuurrrrrr.

What?

> MMUUUUUUUUUURR RRRRRRRRRRRRRR.

> Wookie

Help I'm frightened

> HAHAHAHAHAHA HAHAHAHAHA

So you're Ok with picking me up?

Sure. Just go wank for me on the corner.

Hell no!!

Definitely not my thing!

*wait

You wait!!

There's only one thing for a night like this. A dvd and a big bowl of Nazi ball soup.

OMG

Aaaaaaaaaaaha hahahahahahaha

*Matzo

Oh that's so terrible!!!

Oy vey!

Heck, it's cold. Brrrr. Qubwer is coming.

Oh man, not Qubwer! Beware his frumious snatch and his icy cleats!

New House Stark motto right there. Qubwer is Coming.

Lucky Qubwer!

Hey guess what?
My c**t is coming

OMG!!!! Ewww
wwwwwwwww

*aunt

Going to go leap off
a cliff now

ROFLROFLROFL

I'd forgotten how much my Mom loves buttsex

!!! Buttsex

ARGGG! STOP IT!!

So sorry! *BUTTER

You suck

Is there anything I can do to help?

Well, if you'd pleasure the vacuum around the lounge, that would be a help

...

Oh lord. Not that, I beg you. Just PLEASE RUN it.

Hey, want to go catch that new Clooney - shafts bullocks movie?

~_~ No way that's legal. Or real.

OMG! Sandra Bullock!!

LOL!

Yeah no problem. I'll be there NO No stop that lunch E stop it. No down get down Jesus duck send send

Hahahahahahahahaha

Damned cat.
Damned Siri.

I shouldn't be much longer. Just got to clean my bedroom and vagina

OMG **vacuum

Wow. Holy crap!!!!!

Laughing so much

omg.

Just take care, OK?

Of course. I can hear how terrible it is. The ram is really loud on the metal hooves.

Whoa. EPIC.

LOL! Yeah, it's snorting fire out of its nostrils. It must be as tall as a bus. I think it has acid saliva, too.

LOOOOOOOOOOOOOL

The rain is loud as well, what with the metal roof.

Hey, could you get some immigrant from the chemist on your way past?

Um. Any preference on nationality?

What?

Your immigrant.

Hahahaha Imodium

Uhh, I've got to try to drop the diet sodas again. Wish me luck!

You can do it. I gave up come three weeks ago, and I'm doing OK

HAHAHAHAHAAAAAAA AAAAAAAAAAAAAAAA

OMG!! *coke. Not come! Urgh!

So you've not been come-free then??

It's really lovely down here. And the real Cornish pussies are incredible. So hot and juicy.

ANNA!!!! OMG!!!!

Pasties. FFS.

Speechless

Now I know why Land's End has so many suicides.

For faces, I like to keep my penis really sharp

Crap. Penis

ROFL

pencil. Auto cucumber that, mother ducker

Do you think Leo would like one of those Darth Badger alarm clocks?

... What's that?

Y'know, it's his helmet, but it's an alarm clock.

Darth Badger and his alarming helmet??

Shit. Darth Badger would be a serious badass.

I'm annoyed. I'm fighting the cat. It doesn't want to leave my cock.

O_O The cat wants to stay in the cat.

CAT!

I think maybe you need to take a couple of deep breaths and evaluate your life.

So how was the date last night bro?

How are you doing?

Still really sad :/

Look, come on round. We'll get a big tub of hagen dazs and watch chicks fuck.

OMG.

Hahahaha chick flicks. Stupid phone.

I'm definitely LMAO now! I'll be over in 15

Oh god, they served up these nasty little bits of octopus testicle all chopped up in a red sauce

HOLY CRAP. That's a seriously niche food.

GOD!! That would be even worse. Tentacle was bad enough.

How many octopus would you have to kill to have enough testicles for six people?

... I'm thinking one is still too many

He's being such a jerk. Sure sometimes he's nice, but then he goes all total bastard.

Just ignite him when he's like that

Oh, I wish.
Hahahahahahahaha

*ignore

I think my phone might be telepathic

Wish I could set fire to the asshole!

Maxie was running around for hours, and when he finally came back, he was dragging this enormous dick, and he totally refused to put it down or give it to me for like twenty minutes. There's something not right with that dog.

Omg. STICK

LOOOOOOOOO OOOOLLLLLLLL

Takes after his mistress!!

Gonna stop at the coffee shop on the way up. You want anything?

Oh you're my savior. Can you get me a cinnamon douche latte

I really don't think so!!

sigh. **headdesk**. *dolce

Still laughing. Barista thinks I'm insane

Wise barista.

I think she's a window.

Not window, window.

Well, that clears it up.

WINDOW!

You can see right through her?

Her husband died.

I've decided. I'm not going to take it. There's too many ways things could go wrong, and I'm happy here. So... thanks, but no thanks.

Food call

Enigmatic. You want to do lunch?

No. Well, yes. But no. Good call.

Thanks, but what are you talking about?!

Uhhh so tired. Blue Warrior needs sleep badly. I can hardly do my John today. My boss is not happy.

... By boss, you mean pimp?

WHAT? Urrrh. Not helping. *job

Hahahahaha. You're awesome when you're exhausted.

You think I should get your mother a bunch of flatulence?

ARGH!

I think she gets more than enough of that from my father!!

I mean flowers, obviously.

Oh, _obviously_.

Yeah, I really like her. I'm grinning like an idiot.

She certainly seems to have made a difference for you.

She's like a breath of fresh ass.

That good, huh???

ROFLLLLLLLLLL

*air

Wow, I can't believe your dad has such a cute dick.

WHAT THE HOLY SHIT??

Omg. Whoa.
No nononono. DUCK.

Jesus, Terri. I was about to go call the cops on him!!!

No no, just his pet duck.
No sexual assault.
Hahahahahahaha

God..

Potato bug

What are you getting for dinner? I'm having some meat loaf with mashed parasites.

Oh my god, that's the most disgusting thing I've ever heard!

Ew!

*potatoes

Sick sick SICK!!
I lost my appetite.

It was fun, but I don't think I'm going to see him again.

Yeah?

He's just a bit too old, yknow?

Sure. You like them hung, you dirty thing.

O.O

Noooo! I meant young. I promise I meant young!

I wish you could be here to HIV me to sleep.

I really don't think you mean that

Hahahahahahahaha
Definitely not.
Hug, yes. AIDS, no.

I couldn't believe it. Susan is like foreskin insane.

She's what????? Eww!

OMG!Bwahahahahahaha!!! *freaking!

She's insane, but she's not a pervert

You hope...

You doing OK, sweetie?

A bit better, thanks x

Good. I'm leaving you

oh my god no

NO NO NO!!! Not leaving you.
Leaving NOW.
Leaving work now.

Oh thank God.

I'm going to go be sick now.

You know what night it is?

No?

It's Taliban night!

Da hell?

Oh crap. ITALIAN night.
Meatballs. Garlic bread.
Spaghetti.

No bombs or heroin.

The NSA computers just
went insane on yo ass.

You ready?

Just lemon Parkinsons

Hello

Lemon pork knee pie

Dude, you gotta give up on Siri

Lucky ship

I donut a swan with this phone

This is really damn tough

I found it OK. But it must be really difficult being dickless.

Hey F you!

*dyslexic LOL

Ha ah ha.

I need a peg

?? Just one?

One is plenty

Dare I ask? Is this like some kind of sex thing?

WTF?

Jesus crispy. A pet. Just one PET.

It's been terrible.

Now we have some guy running around the house fingering every hole in sight. It stinks.

Aaa!!!

Holy shit. FUMIGATING. I...

LOOOOOOOL

Can you see if they have any hairball shampoo?

Hm. That might be quite the request.

Oh dear! Hahaha. "Excuse me, I'd like to wash my trichosomes..."

I think they'd bar me from the shop on the spot!

I was thinking of hair-fall, originally...

What time do you think you'll make it?

About 7.30?

Fine. I'll make sure to leave the grave open.

Wow. I'm late, but I'm not Late, y'know?

Gosh. I should hope not! That should have been garage.

Hahahaha

You're my wide

Are you calling me fat LOL?

Hahaha definitely not! I like my nose unbroken :)

Good move :) Your phone better watch it, though!

I may have got you a little thug for Valentine's day :)

Not exactly what I've been dreaming of...

LOL! *thing

Does he come with a little spiked club?

No, a motorbike chain!

You out yet, bro?

No not quite. Just got to chop up my Mom.

Whoa harsh.

She throw out your porn stash again?

Yeah.

*pick

I know I'm being a bum, but is it ok if I leave my suitcase in your cat for another couple days?

Definitely not. She may be a bit of a fat cat, but there's no way it will fit.

Ouch. Nasty. Poor kitty.

Exactly. Bad man.

How about your car then?

Much better!

U OK?

Don't know. Been feeling dick all day.

Hahahahahaha U can't be that bad then!!!

OMG llllooolll! SICK. I need to sue my phone for libel!

That sounds bad :(

Yeah, I'm totally knackered. Been jerking like a monster all day long.

Ugh, filthy bastard. No more sympathy from me.

No no no.

WORKING

Whyyyyyyyyyyyyyyyyyyyy </frankenstein>

I don't know what to believe now...

Sweetie, I'm certain. You are the only fork I want.

Gee.

WHAT? How the hell does that happen? Is this stupid thing totally insane??? How does it get 'fork' from 'girl'??

Hahahahahahahahaha. Your crazy fingers...

Saying. NOTHING.

It could be worse. The vet said that she's got Star Wars. So they can definitely help.

OK. Utterly speechless.

I always knew your cat was Darth Grievous.

Stomach worms.

Dunno which is stranger, your phone or your cat.

Joy of sexts
My new phone is really cool :D :D :D <3
You're welcome sweetie.
I can do three way sex now!!
WHAT??
OMG NO *text *text *text
So sorry, dad. Just a typo. 3-way texts.
...
send whiskey

You all right?

Gah. Not really. Got into a shit-load of trouble at work. Gave this guy a really hard jacking off.

WTF????????

Oh great. No! Goddam phone. I gave this piece of shit a really hard telling off for being a total dick to Stace. A customer. Manager went ballistic.

FM. Shitty. Life.

Think I asshole go to the crow this evening?

I don't think you typed what you think you typed.

Princess Blade, Jim? I'm impressed!

*bride. *show. *should.

I need a neutron.

Yeah. You so do.

Your mom has been having some nasty tooth pain.

We think she's going to need an erection.

Ugh. Thanks for sharing, Dad.

Hm. Extraction.

Get your mind out of the gutter.

You started it...

I aced it. Not to blow my poon horn.

BWAHAHAHA

Yeah. Don't want to blow your poon-horn, dude. You need ribs removed first, or you'll break your spine. Besides, NASTY.

Goddamnit.

It was nice. They made us feel whalecum.

NOT NICE!

*welcome

Why the hell is whale cum in your phone?

Oh God. I mean, why does your phone have that term in it?

Ah, dammit.

My thoughts exactly.

I'm just heading into the office orgy now.

WTF. Not orgy. RIGHT. Office right now.

LOL!!!

I'm calling your director!

I think she's bent over the photocopier...

You gotta try this. Day fuck eight times in a row, real quick. Is it even a word?

Dude, eight times in a row is going to totally wipe you out for more than just a day. You won't be able to walk!

FFS. *SAY.

Hahahahaaa

At a spa actually, being pampered!

Ooo, you lucky thing! I'm Jesus.

Wow! That's a seriously impressive promotion.

Hahahahaha yeah, not sure about the beard though!

If the halo fits...

Dinner disaster

What do you want for dinner?

How about Weinberg?

...

No?

LOLOLOLOLOL!

Hamburger!

Better...

You around at the weekend?

Maybe. I gotta clean up my dad's dick though.

AAA HORRIBLE

*DECK

Now I really wish I hadn't asked!!

Gngngngngngngn

You want I should fix you an aggressive mayo sandwich for lunch?

I prefer calm sandwiches

OMG hahahaha hahahahaha

egg > *agg LOL

ROFL

Whoa! Sorry I asked!

Where did you vanish too?

I left your coffee on Steve's dick

*desk

I am *NOT* drinking anything from Steve's dick

Lol prolly for the best

I'm not sure.

Cmon, you know you want the Hand job.

....!

LOL omg, horrible. Hants job.

Although knowing you...

What about tomorrow?

Even worse. Gotta be up at six for a ten-hour shit at work

HOLY CHRIST!

That would be a truly arse-busting nightmare of a dump. Talk about a bog-rocking turd the size of a submarine!!

Sod that for a game of soldiers! The shift is bad enough!

That's it, I'm ready! You?

Masturbating like a wild thing. Almost there.

HORRIFIED FACE

OMGOMGOMG. Packing. Just packing, I swear.

PMSL!

Swap shop

Can u help me close up tonight?

Sorry, I allready slept with Doug for an early finish tonite

Omg hahaha

Hussey!

Swapped!